ERIC BOGLE
SONGS
BOOK ONE

Wise Publications
London/New York/Sydney

Exclusive Distributors:
Book Sales Limited
8/9 Frith Street,
London W1V 5TZ, UK.

Music Sales Corporation
257 Park Avenue South,
New York, NY 10010. USA.

Music Sales Pty Limited
120 Rothschild Avenue, Rosebery,
NSW 2018, Australia.

This book © Copyright 1995 by Wise Publications
ISBN 0 949789 18 6 (Set)
ISBN 0 949789 19 4
Order No. MS02870

Piano Arrangements by Narelle French
Music Engravings by Rodd Jefferson
Cover Design & Artwork by Serious Business
Printed in Australia by Robert Burton Printers Pty. Ltd.

Music Sales complete catalogue lists thousands of
titles and is free from your local music shop,
or direct from Music Sales Australia Pty. Ltd.
P.O. Box 97, Rosebery, NSW, 2018

CONTENTS

Foreword 5

And The Band Played Waltzing Matilda 6

At Risk 9

Ballad Of Henry Holloway 16

The Gift Of Years 19

Goodbye Lucky Country 22

The Great Aussie Takeaway 25

Hard Hard Times 28

He's Nobody's Moggy Now 30

Just Not Coping 34

Leaving The Land 37

Little Gomez 42

Mirrors 45

Old Friends 52

Never Again/Remember 54

A Reason For It All 59

Rosie 62

Save The Wilderness 66

Safe In The Harbour 70

The Song 73

Welcome Home 76

When The Wind Blows 82

FOREWORD

I believe it was the late great Luke Kelly who first asked me if I had come across the writing of Eric Bogle. Luke knew of my fascination with the 1st World War and told me about the song "And The Band Played Waltzing Matilda" and his intention to record it with the Dubliners. I was immediately jealous, as having Luke sing your songs was to say you had joined the company of the great contemporary writers in the modern "folk song" tradition, I definitely was not sure about Mr Bogle.

I finally got to meet him in his adopted country of Australia in his hometown of Adelaide in 1986 where we had been paired to appear at the Barton Theatre. Eric in his customary unassuming style had agreed to open the show for me. For the next hour or so he ran through a set of original songs (largely unknown to me) that had the audience singing along, or hushed in rapt attention and occasionally laughing out loud at his comic offerings. I was filled with admiration and that night a friendship was formed that has seen us work together in Australia, where we have toured extensively, and Europe and the UK.

Eric's songs are special because the man himself is special, being born and raised in Scotland he was exposed to the living Scottish tradition of songs and music and their ballad influence is evident in his style, he also absorbed the influence of country music and rock'n roll.

Eric's guitar style is uncomplicated and most of his melodies flow from 1st position chords which makes his music accessible though the subject matter may be extremely difficult and controversial. It is this aspect of Eric's writing that I think has flowered because of his love of Australia and its people. Australians "call it like they see it", they have a forthright approach to life and its situations coupled with an enquiring enthusiasm for the truth, and this suits Eric right down to the ground.

He shares this search for honesty, it seems to me that he is unwilling to compromise, he has great compassion for his fellow man but does not suffer fools gladly. He loathes hypocracy and double standards and all of this is reflected in his compositions.

In the selection of material for this Song Book you will see many of these characteristics reflected. The songs are uncompromising in their honesty, almost to the point of pain in some instances. Eric tackles subjects that most people would run a mile from. In this Book there are songs about child abuse, the upsurge in nazism, the death squads to rid the streets of orphans and unwanted children in Brazil, the loneliness of old age, but there are also songs of humour and great compassion, one of my favourites being "The Gift Of Years".

When Eric and I were learning to play the guitar there were hardly any song books about, nowadays there are loads but I bet there aren't many that contain material like this one (except perhaps Book Two).

So if you want songs that look honestly at our present conditions, songs that remind us of our obligation to look at the horrors of the past, or songs to remind us of the need for vigilance to guard and care for our precious planet and the need to look out for each other, then look no further, this is the book for you!

I admire the writing of Eric Bogle and I'm proud to call him my friend.

Ralph McTell London December 1994

And The Band Played Waltzing Matilda

Words and Music by Eric Bogle

gave me a tin hat and they gave me a gun and they marched me aw - ay to the war.

CHORUS

And the band played Waltz-ing Ma - til-da_____ as the ship pulled a - way from the quay.

And midst all the cheers the flag wa - ving and tears, we sailed___ off for

Gal - ip - ol - li.

VERSE 2

And how well I remember that terrible day,
How our blood stained the sand and the water,
And how in that hell that they called Suvla Bay
We were butchered like lambs at the slaughter;
Johny Turk he was ready, he'd primed himself well,
He showered us with bullets and he rained us with shell,
And in five minutes flat he'd blown us all to hell,
Nearly blew us right back to Australia.
CHORUS:
And the band played "Waltzing Matilda",
When we stopped to bury our slain.
We buried ours, and the Turks buried theirs,
Then we started all over again.

VERSE 3

And those that were left, well, we tried to survive
In that mad world of blood, death and fire,
And for ten weary weeks I kept myself alive,
Though around me the corpses piled higher;
Then a big Turkish shell knocked me arse over head,
And when I woke up in my hospital bed,
I saw what I'd done, well I wished I was dead,
Never knew there was worse things than dying.
CHORUS:
For I'll go no more waltzing Matilda,
All around the green bush far and free,
To hump tent and pegs, a man needs both legs,
No more waltzing Matilda for me.

VERSE 4

So they gathered the crippled, the wounded and maimed,
And they shipped us back home to Australia,
The legless, the armless, the blind and insane,
Those proud wounded heroes of Suvla;
And when our ship pulled into Circular Quay,
I looked at the place where me legs used to be,
And thanked Christ there was nobody waiting for me
To grieve, to mourn and to pity.
CHORUS:
But the band played "Waltzing Matilda"
As they carried us down the gangway,
But nobody cheered, they just stood and stared,
Then they turned all their faces away.

VERSE 5

And so now every April I sit on me porch,
And I watch the parade pass before me;
I see my old comrades how proudly they march
Reviving old dreams of past glory,
The old men march slowly, old bones stiff and sore,
They're tired old heroes from a forgotten war,
And the young people ask: "What are they marching for?"
And I ask myself the same question.
CHORUS:
But the band plays "Waltzing Matilda",
And the old men still answer the call,
But as year follows year, more old men disappear,
Someday no one will march there at all.

CODA
Use last verse and tune of Waltzing Matilda

At Risk

Words and Music by Eric Bogle

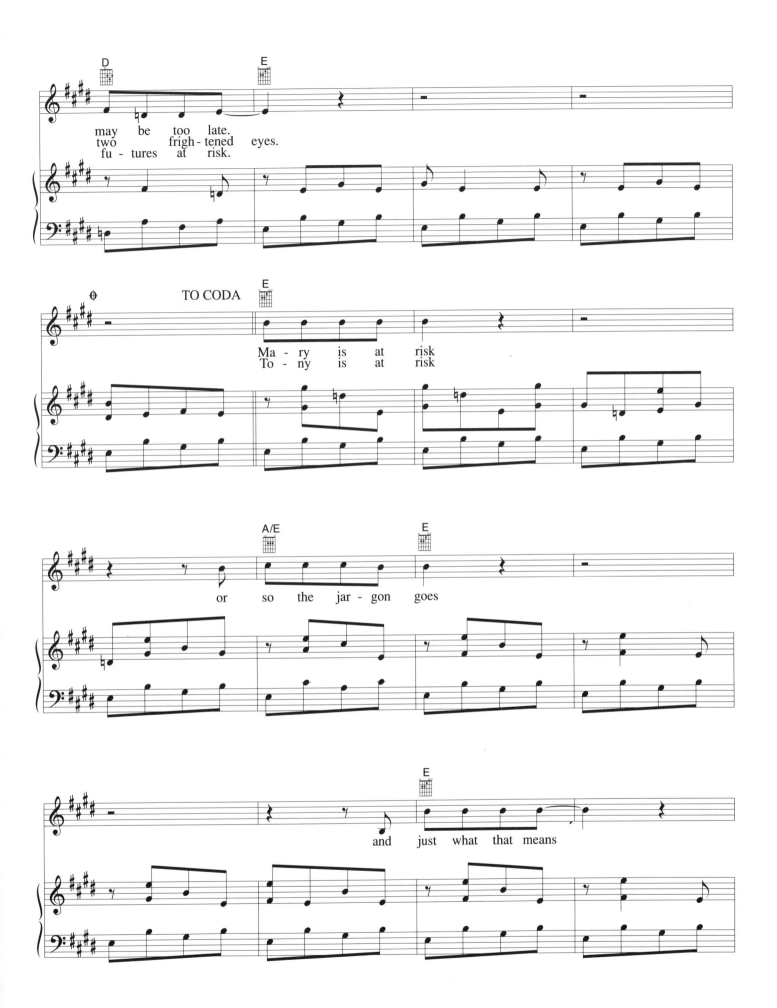

may be too late.
two frigh-tened eyes.
fu - tures at risk.

TO CODA

Ma - ry is at risk
To - ny is at risk

or so the jar-gon goes

and just what that means

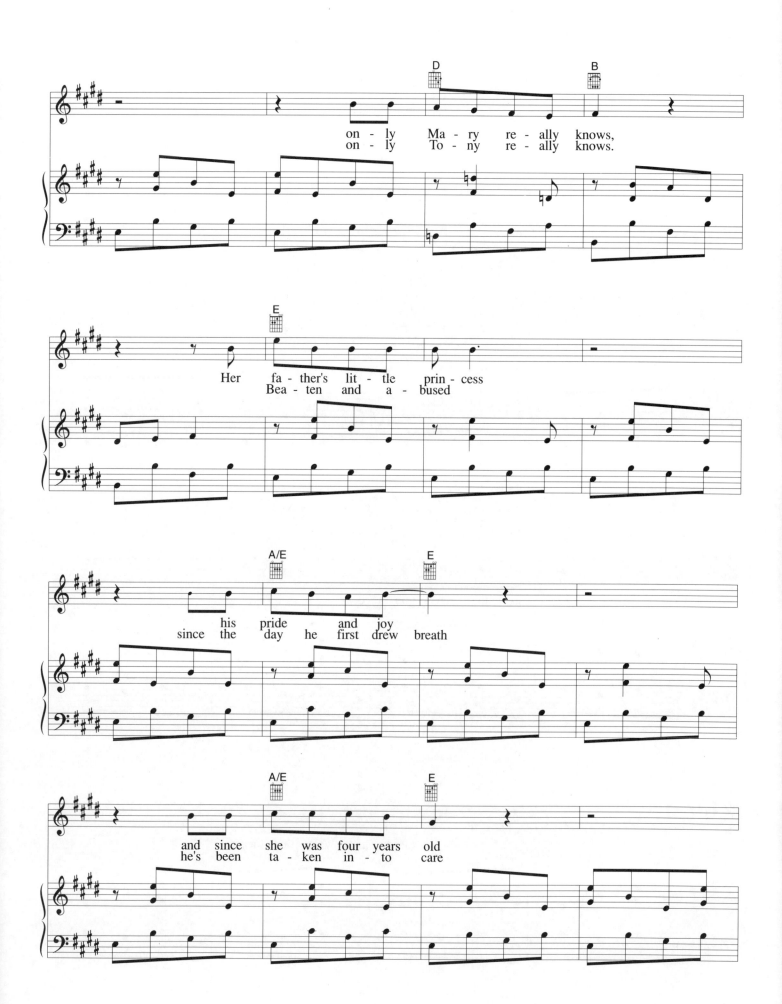

on - ly Ma - ry re - ally knows,
on - ly To - ny re - ally knows.

Her fa - ther's lit - tle prin - cess
Bea - ten and a - bused

since the day he first drew breath
his pride and joy

and since she was four years old
he's been ta - ken in - to care

be - fore his fav' - rite sex - ual toy.
be - fore he's bea - ten to death.

What are we do - ing to our

child - ren what are we do - ing to our -

selves, Deaf and in - diff' - rent to the
From ev' - ry seed that

cries of our young
hate and fear sows

is
a

that what we've be - come?
bit - ter har - vest grows

CODA

What are we do - ing to our child - ren

what are we do - ing to our - selves,

a fa - ding dream on a dy - ing

star

is that all we are?

are?

is that all we are?

15

The Ballad of Henry Holloway

Words and Music by Eric Bogle

Sat-ur - day night and the bar - room is how-lin' with young week-end cow-boys all strutt-in'___ and___ prowl-in'. Drink - ing straight bour-bon and try-in' not to shi-ver___ as it burns down their throat and plays hell with their li-ver. On a small stage in the bar's fur-thest cor-ner sits Hen-ry Hol-lo-way play - in' his

guitar.— Un-der the spot-light, sweat on his face glist-enin'. Sing - in' his

heart out with no-bo-dy listen-in'. Fire in the bel-ly— fire in the soul, am-

bi-tion's a fire that's hard to con - trol. Burn-in' with bright dreams of mo - ney— and

fame, young Hen-ry Hol-lo-way's lost in the flame.—

CHORUS

Repeat to VERSE

VERSE 2
Evyln sits by the stage she's the only one clappin'
With eyes brightly shinin', feet in time tappin'
Face full of love as she watches her man
In his shirt of blue rhinestones she sewed on by hand.
Sweet red lips movin' as she sings along
Joinin' with Henry in his every song
Although she's heard them about one million times
Love is tone-deaf as well as stone blind.
    To CHORUS

VERSE 3
Now the noise in the bar's like a volcano explodin'
But up on the stage young Henry is floatin'
Eyes closed and driftin' through his favourite dream
He sings of places he's never seen
Like Nashville and Memphis, New York and L.A.
You can bet even money he'll get there someday
But if he don't, he just might not care
'Cause when he sings his songs, he's already there.
    To CHORUS

VERSE 4
Saturday night's turned into Sunday mornin'
The bar-room is empty, the bartender's yawnin'
Home go the cowboys with their jeans and their high boots
Come Monday they'll put on their ties and dark suits.
Back to the motel go Henry and Evylin
She falls asleep with her arms wrapped around him
And dreams of motel rooms and cheap crowded bars
Henry lies wide awake and dreams of the stars.
    To CHORUS

The Gift of Years

Words and Music by Eric Bogle

how. The peace that we were fighting for the end to stupid
learned. "Lest we for-get" in the mul-ti-tude as if we ev-er

sense-less war so it could-n't hap-pen to our kids,
ev-er could, so for-give an old man's tears and

thank-you well old mate, it did.
for the years.

(4) But

Goodbye Lucky Country

Words and Music by Eric Bogle

you. Luck-y coun-try how you've changed now no-thing— seems the same, to see you loose your

way fills me with sor-row. You've got to try to tip the scales, you've got to get back on the

rails, or luck-y coun-try will you still be so to-mor-row. (Vs 2) There was a

Luck-y coun-try will you still be so to-mor-row.

Good - bye Luck - y coun - try, who the hell hung that name on

you. When you sink in - to the o - cean, who's a gon-na miss you.

VERSE 2
There was a feelin' in the air that we're going somewhere
We had vigour and vitality and wealth enough to share
Then hard times put us to the test, we held our wallets to our chest
And said that "I'm all right Jack" and to hell with all the rest
    To CHORUS

VERSE 3
What made our country great so history relates
Is how Aussies stuck together and relied upon their mates
Now we care less and less for our neighbours in distress
Each man's a little island in a sea of selfishness.
    To CHORUS

VERSE 4
Nature put proudly in our care a land for all of us to share
We've raped and spoiled and plundered it, and stripped it's bounty bare
And when our consciences said "stay!" we threw our consciences away
For tomorrow's wasted deserts are money in the bank today.
    To CHORUS

Verse 5
So let's all start to care and let's all start to share
Let's reach for new horizons and when we all get there
Let's live at peace between ourselves and one day we might dwell
In a land that's fit for heroes, and you and me as well
    To CHORUS then CODA

The Great Aussie Takeaway

Words and Music by Eric Bogle

I'm an or-din-ar-y Aus-sie bloke cul-tured clean and neat. I do not drink or swear or smoke, but boy, I like to eat! Keep your fil-thy for-eign food, your Greek and Leb-an-ese, Tur-kish and I-tal-ian, French and Viet-na-mese, what makes me mouth wa-ter is-n't an-y one of these, no I like take-a-

VERSE 2
I bought meself a pie the other night down at me local cafe
I was just about to take a bite, when the pie it screamed out "neigh"
And right before me eyes the bloody thing reared up
And took off through the front door like a runaway truck
And the last thing I heard it had won the Melbourne Cup!
But I still like takeaways
    To CHORUS

VERSE 3
So I bought meself some saveloys, though to tell youse all the truth
I wish I'd worn me corduroys, when one of them went "Woof!"
It jumped right off the table and around the room did run
I thought I'd seen it all mate, but the best was yet to come
For it cocked itself against me leg and bit me on the bum!
But I still like takeaways
    To CHORUS

VERSE 4
I bought a hamburger with egg and chips, I had to get a bite somehow
But as I began to lick me lips, my burger screamed out "Meow!"
It scratched me on the nose, I threw it to the ground
It ran up a gum tree, I felt such a silly clown
For the Fire Brigade came and got the stupid burger down!
But I still like takeaways
    To CHORUS

VERSE 5
So I ordered up my favourite treat, steak sandwich on a plate
But before I could begin to eat, my sandwich shouted "Wait!"
"I'm not a buffalo or brumby, cat or dog or grizzly bear
I'm true-blue Aussie kangaroo cooked medium rare"
Then it gave me a salute and sang "Advance Australia Fair!"
But I still like takeaways
    To CHORUS

Hard Hard Times

Words and Music by Eric Bogle

Ending: Ritard last two bars

VERSE 2
Poor Jacky's a stranger in his own land,
Hard hard times.
Livin' in a world he can't understand,
Hard hard times.
Wrecked and drowning in a sea of grog,
His pride and self-respect's been robbed.
Worse off than a white man's dog,
Hard hard times.

VERSE 3
The spirits have fled from the rocks and trees,
Hard hard times.
The land is sick with white man's disease,
Hard hard times.
Their lust and greed does them betray,
They rape the land to make it pay.
The black man just got in their way,
Hard hard times.

VERSE 4
Black man's Dreamtime's dead and gone,
Hard hard times.
White man's Dreamtime marches on,
Hard hard times.
They try to make you civilized,
They just don't seem to realise,
What they touch, they bastardize,
Hard hard times.

He's Nobody's Moggy Now

Words and Music by Eric Bogle

Some - bo-dy's mog-gy ___ by the side of the road, some - bo - dy's

pus-sy ___ who for - got his high-way code. Some - one's fav - 'rite fe - line who

ran clear out of luck when he ran on to the road and tried to ar - gue with a

truck. Yes-ter-day ___ he purred and played in his pus-sy par-a - dise, de - cap-i - ta-ting

twee-tie birds and mas-ti-ca-ting mice. Now he's just six pounds of raw mince meat that

don't smell ve-ry— nice, he's no - bo-dy's— mog-gy———— now.————

All you who love your pus-sy— be sure to keep him in, don't let him ar - gue

with a—truck: the truck is bound to win, and up-on the bu - sy road don't

31

let him play or fro-lic,___ if you do___ I'm warn-ing you it could be cat-a-

stro-phic!___ If he tries to play on the road-way I'm a-fraid that will be

that, there will be one last de-spair-ing "Meow" and a sort of squel-chy

splat! And your pus-sy___ will be slight-ly dead and ve-ry___ ve-ry___ flat, he's

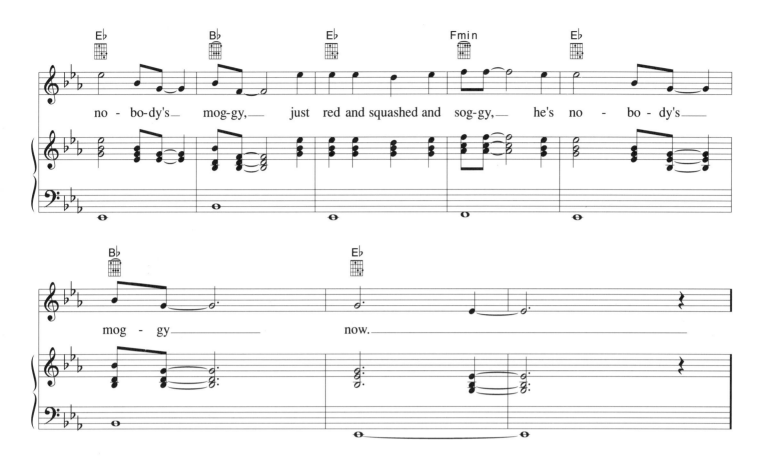

no - bo-dy's__ mog-gy,__ just red and squashed and sog-gy,__ he's no - bo-dy's__

mog - gy_____ now._____

Just Not Coping

Words and Music by Eric Bogle

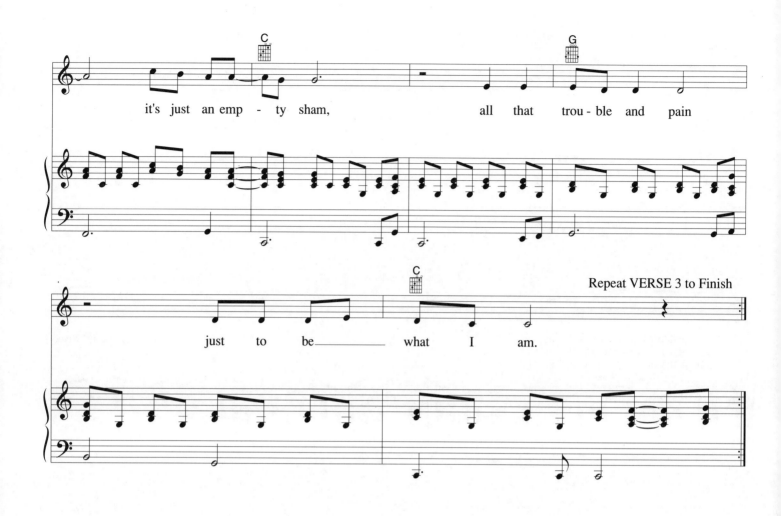

it's just an emp - ty sham, all that trou - ble and pain

just to be_____ what I am.

Repeat VERSE 3 to Finish

Leaving the Land

Words and Music by Eric Bogle

It's time to go   Jen - ny   no need to close the door.
Re - mem - ber when I   brought you here those long   bright years a - go,

What if the dust gets   in the house?   does-n't mat - ter   a - ny - more.
for all that time you've   been my heart,   but this   land has   been my soul.

You and the dust have   been at   war   for   far too ma - ny
The long bright days   are   o - ver now   though   still the heart beats

37

land.

For all I see a - round me sings to me of the past,
It's time to go Jen - ny drive quick - ly down the track,

four gen - er - at - ions loved this land ne - ver thought I'd be the last. All that
we'll ne - ver see what lies a - head if we keep on look - ing back

39

Little Gomez

Words and Music by Eric Bogle

Flynn. At the drop of a som-bre-ro he'd jump up and get stuck in. Ta-king Go-mez out for walk-ies was em-

bar-ras-sing! *(Repeat)* Ta-king Go-mez out for walk-ies was em-bar-ras-sing!

And he said: "Yes, we have no chi-hua-huas, we have no chi-hua-huas to-

day._____ We've Al-sa-tians, Dal-ma-tions, the fruits of a flirt-a-tion 'tween a

43

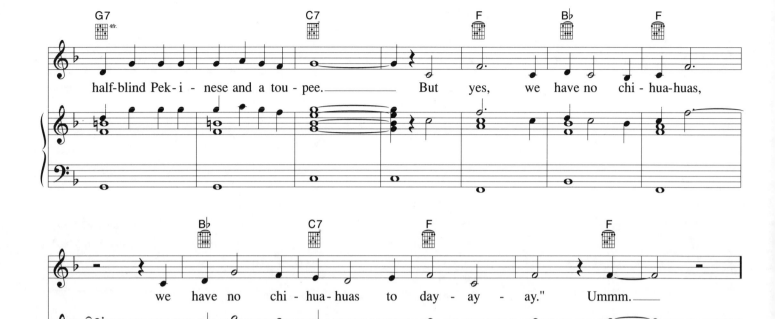

half-blind Pek-i-nese and a tou-pee._____ But yes, we have no chi-hua-huas,

we have no chi-hua-huas to day-ay-ay." Ummm._____

VERSE 2

I remember one day in the park, his tally rose by four,
An enviable score he was amassing.
Two pleased and patient poodles and an outraged labrador,
And a wombat who just happened to be passing!
I tried a hundred ways to curb his carnal appetite,
Kept him on a lead all day, locked him up at night,
I even put some bromide in his chunky meaty-bites
But the only thing that might have worked was Kryptonite! (repeat)

VERSE 3

Then came the fateful day when he tried to consummate
A liason with a St Bernard called Blodwyn.
And even though he was quite clearly fighting well above his weight,
He didn't let that minor detail stop him.
He nearly pulled it off, oh, what an acrobat,
But Blodwyn got bored and down she sat.
They say that after making love you often feel quite flat,
I'm sure that little Gomez would agree with that! (repeat)

VERSE 4

So I buried Gomez in the park, his happy hunting ground,
A sad but fitting finale.
I had to dig a grave that was rather flat and round,
'Cause he looked like a squashed tamale.
But I really missed my wee Chihuahua chum,
So I went down to the petshop to buy another one,
I went in feeling happy, but I came out feeling glum,
Because the man down at the petshop loved corny puns! (repeat)
            TO CODA

Mirrors

Words and Music by Eric Bogle

fear in-stead of trust

and af-ter a while

they're just like us...

Same Tempo with forceful rhythm

To

On this Earth there is a ci - ty in a green and plea - sant coun - try
bless this piece of Pa - ra - dise high on a hill stands Je - sus Christ

where they kill their child - ren, the
ga - zing down with sight - less eyes at this

child - ren of the streets. Free en - ter - prise ex - ter - min - at - ion
dai - ly blas - phe - my A mock - ing mar - ble con - tra - dict - ion

no waste - ful re - ha - bil - it - at - ion,
arms spread wide in ben - e - dict - ion

in our child - ren's eyes, we see mir - rors of our - selves.

Old Friends

Words and Music by Eric Bogle

Shake my hand and say good-bye,
Let's have one drink for Auld Lang Syne,
So shake my hand and say good-bye,

look me square-ly in the eye,
one last toast to hap-py times,
look me square-ly in the eye,

There's no-one here but you and I,
to mem-ories shared they're yours and mine,
if you don't break then neither will I,

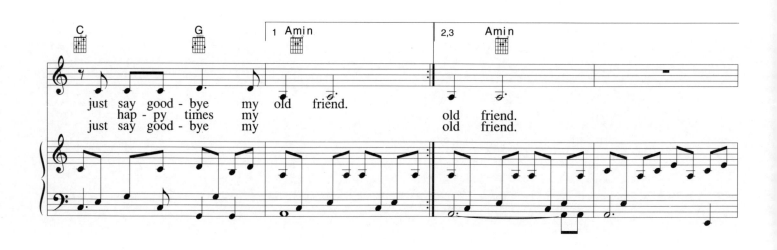

just say good-bye my old friend.
hap-py times my
just say good-bye my

old friend.
old friend.

Never Again / Remember

Words and Music by Eric Bogle

can - cer grew fat and mal - ign re - mem - ber.
whole nat - ions en - slaved and de - based re - mem - ber.

It's ban - ner was a crook - ed cross, re - member? It's des - tin - y a hol - o - caust, re-
Blood and toil and sweat and tears re - member? The night - mare last - ed six long years, re-

mem - ber it's creed was ra - cial pu - ri - ty it fed on fear and bi - got - ry it's
mem - ber the world drowned in a bloo - dy tide of war and death and gen - o - cide

touch was death and sla - ve - ry re - mem - ber. It's hap - pen - ing a - gain it's
fif - ty se - ven mill - ion died re - mem - ber.

CHORUS

can't you see it's hap - pen-ing a - gain.   It's hap-pen-ing a-gain   it's

hap - pen-ing a-gain   can't you see   it's hap-pen-ing   a - gain.

gain.   Can't you see   it's hap-pen-ing   a - gain.
                                                                        (Ne-ver   ne-ver a-gain)

Epilogue   Rubato

I've lived in free-dom all my life,   ne - ver think-ing much a-bout the cost of

57

those who suff - ered and who died so that freed - om's flame would not be lost. I

saw the flame in Sa - chren - hous - en in spite of all, it's burn - in' yet to

all the ghosts who guard the flame. I prom - ise you, I won't for - get Ne - ver ne - ver a-

gain.

A Reason For It All

Words and Music by Eric Bogle

Sum-mer smi-lin' on the ci-ty it's an-oth-er love-ly day in Syd - ney.

Sun-shine pour-in' down like hon-ey in a gol-den wa-ter-fall.

But in the room where Clare is dy-in' no sun-shine sends the sha-dows fly-in',

Tired old peo-ple die a - lone eve - ry day,— don't blame— me I did-n't make it that way that's just how it is,— don't look for a rea-son for it all.

Fine Repeat to VERSE

VERSE 2
Winter weepin' on the city
A wet and windy day in Sydney
Raindrops rollin' fat and heavy,
Down Clare's window-pane.
The rain upon the tin roof beatin'
Disturbs the rats as they are feedin'
Back to their nests they all go creepin'
Leavin' Clare alone again
It's been a long and lonely time since Clare could hear the rain.
CHORUS
Don't talk to me about the meaning of life,
Don't sing your songs that cut like a knife,
I don't want to hear, I don't want to hear it at all.
Lonely old people ain't my concern,
From dust we come, to dust we return
And that's all there is, don't look for a reason for it all.

VERSE 3
Springtime's come at last to Sydney
The flowers are bloomin' in the city,
In all their multi-coloured glory
They rise to greet the year.
Memories in shame recallin'
Footsteps on the front porch fallin'
Voices through the window callin' "Is anybody here?"
Clare Campbell's lost and lonely soul is a long long
way from here.
CHORUS
Don't talk to me about life's seasons
Don't ask me for amswers, don't ask me for reasons
I don't want to hear, I don't want to hear it at all.
From the moment we're born we start to die
And a man can go crazy if he keeps asking why
That's just how it is, don't look for a reason for it all.

VERSE 4
Can't you understand what I'm trying to say
There must be a reason, there must be a way
To make some sense of it, to try to find a reason for it all.
We are not born just so we can die
There must be answer, and we've got to try
To make some sense of it, to try to find a reason for it all.
Final CHORUS*(Sing Chorus to VERSE 3) is sung simultaneously with* VERSE 4

Rosie

Words and Music by Eric Bogle

VERSE 3
I once knew a barren crippled man who stood strong and straight and tall
A bitter heartless loveless man with no pity and no soul
But because his limbs were strong and clean, no one turned aside their face
He was a perfect shining mirror to a perfect human race
   To CHORUS

Save the Wilderness

Words and Music by Eric Bogle

(1) Deep in - side each one of us there is a wild - er - ness,____
(2) This is the age of dark ma - chines that rule our lives and rule our dreams,____

a wild____ and sec - ret place where our souls find re - lease,____
the ta - pe - stry of li - ving green is fa - ding fast to grey,____

where we are chil - dren once a - gain____ li - ving in an un - spoiled land
our fu - ture has been bought and sold,____ we've all been paid in fool's gold,

of earth and trees and sky and peace. Save the wild-er-ness_____ save the
and there's a price we still must pay.

wild-er-ness_____ it's a part of us the part that sets us free,_____ save the

wild - er - ness_____ save the wild-er-ness,_____

if it fades and dies__ then so do we.__

our pre-cious lone-ly frag-ile home. Save the wild-er-ness,_____ save the

wild-er-ness_____ it's a part of us the part that sets us free._____ Save the

wild-er-ness_____ save the wild-er-ness_____

if it fades and dies then so do we._____ Save the we.

Safe in the Harbour

Words and Music by Eric Bogle

Have you stood by — the o-cean — on a dia-mond-hard — morn - ing and felt the hor -

i - zon stir deep in — your soul? Watched the wake of a stea - mer — as it

cut through — blue wa-ter — and been gripped by — a fe-ver — you just can't con - trol?

Oh, to throw off the shack - les_____ and fly with the sea - gulls to where green waves_____ tum - ble be - fore a dri - ving sea wind, or to lie on the deck - ing_____ on a warm sum - mers_____ eve - ning, watch the red sun fall bur - ning_____ be - neath the_____ Earth's rim. (But) to eve - ry sail - or_____ comes time to drop

VERSE 2

Some men are sailors, but most are just dreamers
Held fast by the anchors they forge in their minds,
Who in their hearts know they'll never sail over deep water,
To search for a treasure they're afraid they won't find.
So in Sheltered harbours they cling to their anchors,
Bank down the boilers and shut down the steam,
And wait for the sailors to return with their treasures,
That will fan the dull embers and fire up their dreams.
　　　TO CHORUS

VERSE 3

And some men are schemers who laugh at the dreamers,
Take the gold from the sailors and turn it to dross,
They're men in a prison, they're men without vision,
Whose only horizon is profit and loss.
So when storm clouds come sailing across your blue ocean,
Hold fast to your dreaming for all that you're worth,
For as long as there are dreamers, there will always be sailors,
Bringing back their bright treasures from the corners of the earth.
　　　TO CHORUS

The Song

Words and Music by Eric Bogle

And

Instrumental Solo

74

Welcome Home

Words and Music by Eric Bogle

in a heart - beat she was in his arms. Wel - come
Ann - ie wait - ed for his wounds to heal.
them the war was ov - er at last. Wel - come

home boys wel - come home don't you know you've been gone too

long._____ we're just so Did you won - der ov - er there when you were
glad that you sur - vived and on - ly

don't you know   you've been gone too   long.   What   you   went
                                                                            May   the

through   in   Vi - et - nam,   we can't be - gin   to un - der - stand   but to
years   bring   you re - lease   as   the me - mor - ies   de - crease   may   you

each   and   ev' - ry   man   wel - come   home.   Wel - come
find   some   kind   of   peace

Repeat Final Chorus and Fade

When the Wind Blows

Words and Music by Eric Bogle

Repeat in this manner
(ie 1st bar of Verse overlaps with last 2 bars of previous verse)
(Last time repeat "When the wind blows")

VERSE 2

The Shadows are advancing, over all the earth they're dancing,
And everywhere they dance they're bringing death.
All the bright uneven pages that we've written through the ages
Shall vanish in the Shadow's poison breath.
The storybook will close
When the Wind Blows.

VERSE 3

Suddenly I'm frightened, how I wish this room were lightened,
Can no-one light a candle in this dark?
For I hear the sullen murmur of far off threatening thunder,
Feel it's menace chill me to the heart.
Where can I hide where can I go?
When the Wind Blows.

VERSE 4

There is no-one that can save you, nowhere that you can run to,
No shelter in a world that's gone insane.
In this world that we created in our arrogance and hatred
We'll stand naked 'neath the gentle deadly rain.
But there will be no rainbows
When the Wind Blows.

VERSE 5

In this darkness I am trembling, this night seems never ending,
It seems the morning sun will never rise.
The crashing of the thunder splits my head asunder,
And the lightning burns and eats into my eyes.
Oh how the darkness grows!
When the Wind Blows.

VERSE 6

In a thousand searing flashes, the world shall turn to ashes,
Whirling like a burning coal in endless space.
This good earth we did inherit we shall leave a smoking desert,
A headstone for the heedless human race.
To mark our final throes
When the Wind Blows.

VERSE 7

Oh, I must be dreaming, for I thought I heard a screaming,
Like a billion lost souls falling into hell.
In a thousand tongues bewailing, at indifferent fate all railing,
Each one calling on their saviour as they fell.
We shall reap what we did sew
When the Wind Blows.

VERSE 8

You can call upon your saviour if you think that is the answer,
But you've called on him so many times before.
Call on Allah, Bhudda, Jesus, I doubt if they will hear us,
For we've let the devil loose now hear him roar!
Hell shall overflow
When the Wind Blows.